A WALK WITH FAITH

By

Tujuana Talia Lewis

Dedication

I would like to dedicate this book to two significant little women in my life, my daughters Tivon "T" (age 10) and Jazzlin "Jazz" (age 7). Mommy wouldn't be half the woman she is today if it wasn't for you two beautiful girls. You girls give Mommy the strength, motivation, and determination to make a better life for all of us. I thank you for the patience and tolerance that you guys have for me. I know I can be a bit much and hard on you both at times, but I want nothing more than for you to succeed in life!

I live my life as an example for you to follow. My heart's desire is for you to say, "Mommy I want to be just like you!" You will go through your journey in life, and the testing of your faith, but I pray that my faith walk has and will encourage you never to be afraid to follow your dreams and trust God every step of the way. God got us! Like we say, "Teamwork makes the dream work!" We are a team and will always have each other's backs. Mommy is here to support you and your dreams 100%! Nothing is too hard if you believe. You can do all things through Christ who gives you the strength. Always shoot for the stars, don't forget to enjoy the view on the way up. I love you forever, big girls!

Love,
Mommy

Review

"There comes a time in everyone's life when they must sail on the old ship of Zion. By this, I mean take your walk with faith. In this book, *A Walk with Faith*, the author has invited you to board her ship of faith and sail through currents of testing, trials, and personal testimonies and she tenaciously wades through high flood waters and fails victoriously in her pursuit to "fit in." This young author's transparency, as well as her undaunting faith in Christ, is sure to encourage the lowly at heart, strengthen the weary, and inspire the uncertain. This book is a must-read for anyone who is fighting the good fight of faith. What kind of vessel are you? Are you ready to strap up your boots and take a walk with faith? All Aboard!!!"

Dr. Crystal Hudson, DCE
Greater Faith Ministries of Augusta Int'l
Augusta, GA

Contents

Foreword

My name is Juliet Reid, a retiree from the Circuit Court of Cook County/Officer of the Courts, specializing in Domestic Violence. I would not have been able to succeed in my education or my professionalism without God in my life.

The author of this book is my granddaughter Tujuana Lewis, whose life has been a living sacrifice for God. I feel that she has been anointed by God to be an inspirational speaker, by giving courage to the broken hearts and strength to the weak.

This author has been through dark days, dissatisfactions and disappointments; however, she was able to master those difficulties with the Grace and Mercy of God through the Holy Spirit that lives in her. To see this young author's transformation and determination is a real blessing.

The purpose of this book is to show how God's Holy Spirit can change people's outlook on life, and how he can turn a negative into a positive. From the mouth of my deceased pastor, "God can make a straight line with a crooked stick." God can help all humanities regardless of race, color or creed because God is Love and cannot fail. God can do for you as he has done for Tujuana. Praise be to God!

Grandma aka "Grandma Feedie Cakes"

In Loving Memory Of

~*Juliet Reid*~

March 26, 1936 - August 15, 2018

I dedicate this book to my precious grandmother, whom I love and adore with my whole heart. My grandmother gave me hope when I felt weak. She encouraged me when I needed it and was there every time I called on her. Words can never express the sorrow in my heart, but my peace lies in knowing we will be back together. Grandma, your death was sudden to those who loved you, but on time to your God who called you. Your foreword makes this book even the more special, and I'm glad your words will never die. Rest peacefully my angel, you've earned your wings!

Acknowledgements

Writing this book has been a desire of mines for quite some time now, and it would not have been possible without the help and assistance of some significant people.

Dr. Bola Charles King-Rushing was my English professor at Oxnard College. I reached out to him about editing my book and he did not hesitate to help me. I would like to thank him for taking the time to edit my book and getting it done in a timely manner. I want to thank my photographer Shervan Tavernier who has done a fantastic job with my photos. I didn't have to take too many pictures before landing the perfect ones. I want to acknowledge my spiritual dad and mom, Dr. LeMarcus and Crystal Hudson for their guidance and belief in me to make this book possible. I want to thank my mentor Prophetess Ceretta Smith for always pushing me to do my best and never settle for less, as well as for all the tips on how to write a book. I also want to thank Pastor Dan and Joanie Fuller for loving me back to life and showing me my true potential when I doubted myself. Thank you to everyone who has had a positive influence in my life. Your love and support mean the world to me. Thank you!

Introduction

I am simply here to inspire, encourage and motivate you to pursue your God-given purpose, by simply being you. I'd first like to give all the Honor and Glory to my Savior, rock, and strength, my Jesus Christ! I am so in love with a man named Jesus. There hasn't been one person on planet earth who has taken care of and has loved me better than he has. I only know that because I have allowed him to have complete control over my life. I have known for some time now that I am not in control of my life. I have handed it over to him, and he directs it his way. It doesn't always seem favorable, but it turns out in my favor every time.

I am going to take you with me on this journey showing how faithful God is to his word, and how he does what he says he's going to do. My hope and prayer for this book is that you not only walk away knowing my story, but that you would apply these same faith principles to your life. When you learn to live a life trusting God one hundred percent, you have stepped into a realm that cannot be ignored, a space where the devil has no choice but to back off. A place where peace is on you, so that when you should be panicking, you're instead smiling and going on about your day forgetting the trials you're facing. That is the life that I live, and I want to show you how to live that same life.

I hope you're ready to be inspired, encouraged, and motivated to excel in your faith, because that's what this book will bring. God does not play favoritism to those who serve him, so he doesn't choose to do for one what he wouldn't for another. He is faithful to do for you as he has done for me. I know it like I know my name. He will do it for YOU TOO!

Chapter 1

My Faith Journey Begins

~What a Turning Point~

I can't say that I grew up in the church; although we did go when I was a young girl until about the age of eight. My parents, however; did grow up in the ministry. That is how they met, in church. My grandfather was a pastor and served in ministry as long as I can remember, so it's safe to say I knew about God and knew there was a God. However, to have a personal relationship with him was not a topic of discussion in my family. Prayer was talked about in my household, but the evidence and fruit of walking with the Lord weren't

1

present. In fact, my dad found himself on the streets smoking crack cocaine and trying to sell things out of our house, while my mom did her best to provide for my brother, sister, and me.

When my sister was in the twelfth grade, she was introduced to the idea of joining the Navy. One of her friends mentioned it to her, and the next thing we knew, she had talked to a recruiter and decided that this was what she wanted to do. My mom had no idea my sister had made the decision. My sister came home one day and, in passing, said to my mom, "I'm joining the Navy," and was going to continue with her day like it was nothing. My mom, on the other hand, was having a complete confusion of a moment and called my sister to come back. Although my mom was not jumping for joy, she did end up supporting my sister's decision to join the Navy.

After seeing my sister go through the process of being prepared for the military, I realized then that that was what I also wanted to do. My sister is two years older than me, so even when I decided to go, I was still too young. I had to wait until I turned eighteen and graduated from high school. Around this time, I'd never even considered going to college. So, the military was my only option. Joining the Navy changed my life forever. At this point, I didn't know that I was led by God, but I know now, that He was behind this decision the entire time.

After graduating from boot camp in Great Lakes, IL, I was sent to "A" school in San Antonio, TX for (what was supposed to be eight weeks) 4 months. Now that I am out of my mom's house and out of strict boot camp going to Texas felt like freeeee-dom. It wasn't complete freedom because we were on a Phase system and depending on your phase, depended on how much freedom you had. Being on my own was the first time I had experienced peer pressure at its finest. I have always been a strong-minded person, and it was hard to talk me into doing something I didn't want to do. If I did it, it's because I wanted to. However; I met my challenge in "A" school.

One night my friends decided they wanted to go to the club, which they could do because of the phase they were on. I, on the other hand, was only in phase two and had a curfew. They decided to talk me into sneaking out and going with them, and honestly, I didn't want to go because I was so scared. I tried arguing back and forth with them until I finally gave in. They convinced me I wouldn't get caught because they knew people that do it all the time and never got caught, which a few of them were sneaking out again that same night, so they put my little nerves at ease. On top of that, I had never been to a club at this point, so I did want to go with them deep down inside.

I promise the whole night I was very jittery. I wasn't sure what being convicted meant at the time, but I now know that the Holy Spirit was beginning a new work in me then. I was full of conviction and knew it wasn't right, but I just kept going with the flow and trying to have a fun night. About one hour after getting to the club, I would never forget the phone call that I got from my friend Bria. (I'll be using alias names to protect the identity of people who have no idea they are a part of this book). She called all hysterical, "Hilliard, they just called an all-hands surprise muster!" In the military everyone is on last name basis. An all hands muster is just taking the roll call of everyone. They called everyone out of their rooms and took roll. A surprise all hands muster, is just what it sounds like, a darn SURPRISE. Out of all nights they could have done that, it happened on the night I wanted to be a follower.

Now mind you, nobody had a car to rush us back; we rode in a cab to get there and now had to call and wait on another one to get back to base. I can't remember who rode back with me, but it seemed like forever for the cab to arrive. About 45 minutes after getting the first call, I was still at the club trying to get back. I get a second phone call: "Hilliard, they just called another one!" At this point, I knew I was doomed. I think I cried and everything, as just about every emotion came over me.

We finally got back to base. As soon as the cab pulled up, we jumped out and ran to the dorm to sneak back in the window. The taxi dropped us off in the back of the building, so you couldn't see us creeping back in. It was quite a few people who snuck out, and it was a success! We made it back, and I took my tail straight to sleep, no harm, and no one was caught ... or so I thought.

The very next day, me and everybody else who didn't answer when their names were called last night, were called into the office with our Chief and 1st Class Petty Officer. I walked in there shaking in my boots (literally). I think about this situation now and feel so dumb about the whole thing. It was not worth it to me. I couldn't even enjoy myself. I was nervous the entire time, and I wasn't a drinker, so it's not like I at least got drunk and felt a false sense of it being worth it.

No, it was the stupidest thing I've done. I believe God has allowed situations like this, for me to realize how much I do not fit in and cannot do what everybody else does.

My mom and dad had nicknames for me when I was little: "Do" and "Don't." To this day, my mom calls me "Do," and my dad calls me "Don't." The names just stuck, because I always did the opposite of what I was told. As I said, if I wanted to do it, I was going to do it no matter what anyone said. I was never a troublemaker or an evil child, just a little rebel at times.

Although that rebel side of me kept me in trouble as a little girl, it serves its purpose now that I'm an adult. I look for opportunities for someone to tell me I can't do something; I will do it to show you that I can. I guess you can call it a competitive side, but I'm always up for the challenge and charge that energy to pursuing my dreams and purpose for my life.

When I went into that office, they asked a simple question: "Where were you last night?" In my eighteen-year-old mind, I thought I could lie my way out of it. They didn't go in my room, so I just figured I'd say I'm a hard sleeper and didn't hear them (yeah, right). They saw right through that bologna of a lie and sent me right on to XOI. XOI is the Executive Officer, where you appear before going to the Commanding Officer at Captain's Mast where you receive your punishment (or sentence, that's what it felt like).

Even while at XOI, I believe I had a chance not to have gotten in trouble if I would have just told the truth and took responsibility for my actions. When my Chief asked me where I was at, I believe if I would have been honest and just said I snuck out and apologized, I don't think they would have taken further action. Same thing at the XOI board. That was nerve-wracking because I was in front of a board of people and they all took turns interrogating me. I remember after I explained what happened, the Executive Officer asked me a question: "So, it was your friends' fault that you went out, they forced you to sneak out?" I had to take responsibility for my actions. My friends pressured me, but I wanted to go as well, and that's what I should have said. At that time, this was the first time I had ever been in trouble with the LAW and didn't know how to handle it, so I thought to tell them what they wanted to hear.

Looking back now, I realize they wanted Honor, Courage, and Commitment, which are the Navy's core values. I failed myself, my friends, and my superiors by lying and not taking responsibility for myself.

I would never forget how I felt. The shame and embarrassment that came with my punishment were again not worth it. However, what I learned from that situation is never to lie, and no matter the cost and consequences honor your team, dare to stand for what is right and commit to the right things always. Even though I still wasn't serving God at that point, it was a turning point in my life. That is what I believe catapulted me to serve God. It was a year after that situation that I gave my life over to God. God seriously works in mysterious ways!

If I had not got in trouble, I'd have gone to a ship, where I wouldn't have been surrounded by the right people to guide me in the things of God. My punishment consisted of 45 days restriction, a demotion in rank, and loss of one and a half month's pay. They took my money for a month and a half and locked me in this room for much of the time. I had arrived in San Antonio, TX in January of 2005. I was supposed to leave the beginning of March but stayed until April. When it came time for me to finally leave "A" school and go to my first duty station, the only place that was available was New Orleans, LA, and that is where my life was transformed forever.

Chapter 2

Hurricane Katrina

~I Will Never Forget~

New Orleans, Louisiana, gave me great memories. When I first got there, I had no idea that my friend Bria was at the same base. I remember one of my first days there; the barracks manager called a muster for everyone to come outside. I believe they were doing room inspections and we had to go out to clean up. I guess people started mentioning my name when she realized I was there. I ended up running into her. I'm not sure exactly where I saw her, but I remember being so happy that I knew somebody there. Although we were both Culinary Specialists, we didn't work together. I worked in the Galley (kitchen), and she worked at a Squadron. We would see each other either after work or on weekends. I am so grateful that we never lost contact and are still friends to this day!

Before arriving in New Orleans, the only other club I'd ever went to was the one in Texas. Back home we had what we called house parties and King Center parties. The Martin Luther King Jr. Center was a recreational center for the youth, and now and then, they would throw parties. That was as far as parties as I experienced. I think that's kind of funny that New Orleans, home of Mardi Gras, was the place I encountered the real club life for the first time, and it was lit!

My friends and I would go to the club on most weekends and some Thursday nights. Club Utopia on Bourbon Street was our spot. I would go down there by myself at times. I know God has always had his hand on my life, because downtown New Orleans is not a place a young girl should be by herself unless you're from there—and you could tell I wasn't from there. I was only nineteen years old but was never scared or worried about anything, and anything could have happened to me. I was a dancer, and dancing is my life! I was a hip-hop dancer, so I would dance battle every time I went. I was so known and so cool with the bouncers that whoever went with me got in free. I didn't have to pay to get in, because they knew me as the dancer and they were making bets on me. I wasn't a drinker at first, so I was the designated driver whenever I went out with my friends. Of course, everyone wanted to ride with me because they knew they were getting there and back, safe and sound.

New Orleans is also where I met the Kennedys, the couple who forever changed my life. I worked with Maurice Kennedy at the Galley, and he would always minister to me about God. Later, I met his beautiful wife, Lydia Kennedy. One of the very first conversations I had with Mr. Maurice was of him asking me did I know Jesus and what denomination I was. I did know Jesus and knew that I was Baptist because that's what my family was, but that's all I knew. He also asked me about the disciples and some other stuff about the Bible that I didn't know. We would have those conversations quite often at work, and I believe I got more and more curious to know more about Jesus.

He ministered to me for about three months before I decided to finally go to church with him and his family. I walked in church on Sunday, August 21, 2005, for the first time, and I gave my life to Christ that Sunday. I remember being so happy about my new-found relationship with Christ, but unfortunately it was short lived. The following weekend is when mine and so many other lives changed forever.

I arrived in New Orleans the same year the devastating Hurricane Katrina hit. I will never forget that experience. It was Sunday evening on August 28, 2005; we were at work keeping an eye on the hurricane and waiting on instructions for the evacuation process. Sometime that afternoon, they announced that there was a mandatory evacuation call to the city. When my supervisors received the word for us to evacuate, they told us to drive towards Houston, TX. I went to my barracks room, grabbed what I could and headed out with Bria. I'm happy I gassed up the day before; the gas stations were packed to the point that they start running out of gas. Getting out of the city was absolute chaos. New Orleans to Houston should only take about five hours. It took us approximately nineteen hours to finally make it to Houston.

When we got there, we found a motel room for the night. We thought we would be heading back the next day, so we stayed in the motel to wait out the hurricane and get further instructions from my Chief. We watched and followed that hurricane all night. The next day, August 29, is when the storm hit. After realizing we were not getting back to New Orleans, we got the phone call to go home and wait until further notice to return. We got up and had to drive another seventeen hours to Chicago. Bria was also from Chicago, so I took her home and then headed to my mom's house in South Bend, Indiana. Bria was learning how to drive at the time, and I was teaching her. I was so tired that I had to make her drive on the highway, and although she was scared, I'm so proud of her, she did it! We stayed home for about a week and a half on free leave, until we got called to come back.

The bridges to enter New Orleans were still broken, so we were told to go to Memphis Naval base and from there we would catch the government plane to New Orleans. We stayed a night at the barracks and the next morning, headed out. Bria and I were split up when it was time to go, and I had to stay an extra night in Memphis because of the plane's max capacity. There was so much going on; it was all confusing. The plane flew to Virginia to pick up more people, and we ended up staying a couple of days there due to some mix-ups of the flight schedules. We didn't get to New Orleans until about four or five days later, and I eventually met back up with Bria.

I can't even begin to explain the sight we met flying back in. The city was in absolute shambles and entirely under water. They call New Orleans a "bowl." The Naval base where I was stationed is in Belle Chasse, LA, which sits above the bowl, so it didn't have any water damage, but it did suffer from wind damage. There were trees, branches and other stuff everywhere. Windows broke, and the electricity was messed up throughout the base. We were without cars for a couple of weeks. Even if we had had our cars, we couldn't leave the base. The entire command was on lockdown for about a month.

As Culinary Specialists we were one of the last groups to leave the base before the hurricane and one of the first to come back after the storm. The base was filled with people from different branches of the military as well as various government rescue teams. I'm not sure how many people we fed in a day, but it was in the thousands for breakfast, lunch, and dinner. We were on shifts and worked twelve- to fifteen-hour days. We didn't get a day off for about two weeks.

I salute everyone who had anything to do with that devastating event. So many people came together to accomplish the goal of rescuing and helping wherever was needed. I'm grateful for the experience and having the opportunity to participate in taking care of our men and women who went out to do the hard jobs.

During all that madness, it is safe to say I never stepped foot back into a church. The devil used that time to try and take me out, too. Up until this point, I never had drunk alcohol and cared nothing about it. New Years of 2006, I went back home to visit and drank alcohol for the first time with my cousin, brother, and his friends. If it wasn't for Hurricane Katrina, I believe I would have never known the taste of alcohol.

I cared nothing about alcohol before because I saw the damage it can cause. The smell of alcohol irritated me. My dad was a drinker, and when he drank, he thought he was superman, doing stupid things. I remember when I was about ten years old and witnessed one of my dad's many stunts when he was drunk. At the house we were living in was a parking lot next to it. Well, my dad was feeling himself this night. He got in his car and started doing donuts in the parking lot and yelling out of the window as if he was on a joy ride. It was scary to watch because he had no cares in the world. It was only by the Grace of God that he did not run into a building or into our house. My sister and I were looking out of the side window of the house watching his foolishness play out. That is just one of the many life-threatening moments I witnessed with him and alcohol.

After the hurricane I started working at this beauty shop braiding hair for extra cash and just to stay busy. The stories that I heard about some of the incidents due to the hurricane makes my stomach turn every time I think about it. There was a lady who had two children and couldn't swim with them both, so one of them drowned. I can't even begin to imagine having to witness my baby drowning. I didn't have any children at that time, but it made me sick just knowing someone had to go through that. There were some other stories that you wouldn't even believe unless you were there. After dealing with all of that for them couple of months, going back home New Year's and drinking alcohol didn't seem so bad after all. That is where my life took a turn for the worst, but ultimately led to my salvation.

Chapter 3

My Salvation

~The Lord Rescues His Baby Girl~

I got back to New Orleans and informed my friends that I drank now. They were too excited to celebrate with me. Although I was drinking, I never drank beer, or anything hard. I liked fruity drinks. My favorite was a pineapple amaretto that I would get every time I went out. I never got intoxicated to the point of not knowing my surroundings and was still ok to drive, so I would consider myself to have been a responsible drinker. Except on my twentieth birthday that April of 2006.

21

That birthday was the final straw for me and my very short-lived drinking days. I honestly thank God for that. I have never been a person to get hooked or stuck on anything. I could and would try something and keep it moving. I smoked weed and black-&-mild's for about two months my junior year in high school until my basketball coach put me in a game all four quarters, and by half-time, I thought I was going to die. I coughed my lungs up so hard that I told myself, I am not smoking anything else. I realized that I'm an athlete and this is not me.

My birthday was on a Saturday that year, and I wanted to go to church the next day. My friend Teka threw me a party at her apartment, and some of my friends came over to celebrate with me. I don't understand how I started drinking and still wasn't of age yet. After we kicked it at her house, everybody wanted to go to the club, so we headed there. I got drunk for the first time. I wasn't too tore up to where I didn't know my surroundings, but I remember stumbling all the way back to my friend's apartment. The next morning, I realized I didn't like what I saw or felt. I had a hangover, my head was hurting, my hair was all over my head, and I was mad for not making it to church. I felt like a failure. I knew there was more to life than what I was experiencing, and I wanted better, I was over it.

That same month my brother was getting into some trouble back home and needed to get away. I sent for him to come to stay with me so that I could get him away from the drama. Although I hadn't been to church since last August, Mr. Maurice never stopped ministering to me about God and inviting me to church. He and his wife would ask me to their house and continue to spread the love of Christ with me. When he found out I was sending for my brother to come to stay with me, he started encouraging me, even more, to go to church and bring my brother. So, May 18, 2006, I went back to church with the Kennedys for Thursday night Bible study. They were at a different church by this time, due to the hurricane wiping away and scattering the other church. This church was in Slidell, LA, about forty minutes from base, but I was so ready for change that distance did not matter to me.

When I walked into that church, I felt a peace that I hadn't known before. The word was excellent, the atmosphere was great, and I felt like I just met a group of people that had suddenly become my family. I felt a sense of belonging and acceptance.

Although I gave my life to God at that moment, my brother was not ready, and I didn't understand that. The enemy brought so much division between my brother and me that I had to send him back home because we were fighting and arguing so bad. I felt he should want God the way I did, not understanding that he had his process that God must take him through, and in God's perfect timing He would bring him to the throne.

I am happy to say that today my brother is a devoted man of God. He's married with two beautiful children and serves in the ministry with all his heart. He lives a sober life and rocks his brand, #soberlife. My brother has been rapping since he was a little boy; music is his life! God has turned his lyrics around to glorify his name and shame the devil, and he and his wife are doing amazing things for the Kingdom of God. Glory to God! Since going to church that Thursday evening of 2006, I never turned back, and have been living a life devoted to God ever since.

The beauty shop I was working at had barbers as well and I was in the same room with them, braiding hair. I knew how to braid because my house was the beauty shop growing up and my mom worked at a beauty shop when I was little. I picked up some hair skills just from being around my mom and sister. There was a man who would come in the shop to get lined up by the barbers. He had long hair, but I never braided it; he always wore a ponytail. I would see this man all the time, and we'd speak, but he never asked me out. When I got saved is when he decided to make a move.

I ended up giving him my number, and he asked me to go to the club with him. At this point, I was learning a lot of new things about living holy, so I was done with the club. I told him I just got saved and I couldn't club anymore. He convinced me that I didn't have to do anything, just go dance and have a good time. It sounded innocent enough, so I took him up on his offer. He invited me in June, the month after I got saved. Just two months prior I was in the club all the time dancing and shaking a tail feather on the stage. When he took me to that very club, my club, Club Utopia, I had a Holy Ghost experience. It was a Holy Ghost set-up.

When we got there, I remember looking at the girls on the stage doing the very thing I was doing and dressing the same way I was, and I got sick to my stomach. The Lord told me just as clear as day, "This is not what I have for you, I have better for you." Of course, I didn't know what I was feeling, I just knew I didn't want to be there and that it was time to go. I had to tell ol' boy to take me home. We were there for maybe twenty minutes, and I was ready to go. He thought it was just that club, so he thought to take me to a little hole in the wall club somewhere in the seventh ward, it was the same feeling. I stayed with him for a little bit, but he knew I was antsy and wanted to leave, so he took me back home. That was the last time I ever stepped foot in a club. I know some people who say there's nothing wrong with going to the club while living for God. I am in no position to judge anyone, I just know the experience the Lord took me through, and I can't go against my convictions.

When I started going to church, I learned some values that were instilled in me that I didn't know before. I learned about tithing and giving of your finances, as well as how to dress modestly and not to let it all hang out. One of the first Sundays I went to church I wore this little skirt and thought I was cute. I figured it was a skirt, so it's ok. I knew something was wrong because I didn't feel comfortable. Although no one said anything to me, it was the Holy Spirit that started working on me, and my discernment started getting stronger. I changed the way I was dressing from that moment forward.

I also learned the value of my body and how it is holy to God, and because of that, sex is only between a husband and wife. I remember hearing that when I was little, but it wasn't forced on me by my parents, so I thought no more of it. My mom just told us to tell her when we were ready to have sex. Of course, I wasn't stupid enough to ever tell her that, because it was a set-up. So, she never knew when I did. Unless that mother instinct kicked in and she just never said anything to me.

At the time I started going to church I did have a boyfriend who was also in the Navy and got stationed in Japan. We met at "A" School. I couldn't talk to him unless he called because of the distance. When my boyfriend at the time I got saved finally called me, I had to tell him that we couldn't have sex anymore because I'm now living for God. He was livid when I said it to him. I don't know what was

27

happening in the spirit, but he made the comment that his mom just got saved and I remember him saying, "What's wrong with y'all?" He didn't want to wait for me, so he left me. I talked to my pastor about it, and he explained that sex was all he wanted from me. It broke my heart, and I was crushed, but I accepted it and moved on with my life. He did call me a few months later and apologized, wanting to work it out. By the time he called back I was over him and said I didn't want to do this anymore. I haven't heard a word from him to this day.

My pastor at the time told me I was the fastest convert he had ever seen. That's not to say that I was or am perfect by any means, but at the time I didn't struggle with what I learned about God, or with what the pastor told me. I think also, the pastor was one of the first men in my life who had an honest interest in me and my salvation and not in the way I looked. I felt like men always looked at me like a snack, and it was nice to have a father figure in my life. He and his wife became the parents I never had. With all of that, I held on to the words of my pastor, which is why God cut my time short in New Orleans. I believe the pastor might have become God in my life. I mean that man could have told me that God said to jump off a bridge and I would have done it. Ok, maybe that's a little dramatic, but that's just how serious I was about serving God. I was what you call "Sold Out for Christ" and still am! I am grateful for the values that were instilled in me.

I was only at that church for about six months before I got stationed in Washington, DC. The military cut my orders short in New Orleans because the Galley was getting contracted out to civilians and the Culinary Specialists were no longer needed. When I got to D.C., I found a great church in Woodbridge, VA which became my home church for the three years I was stationed there. That was also about a forty-five-minute drive, but again, distance means nothing to me when it comes to serving God. After only being in D.C. for three months, I met someone who would become my husband just two months later.

Chapter 4

Marriage & Divorce

~ Why ~

U pon arriving in D.C., it was exciting to see another new place. I was now at my second duty station and feeling like I could take on the world. As a Culinary Specialist, your secondary duty was working in the barracks. There wasn't a galley for military cooks on the base because of the contracts run by civilians, although I did a little work with the cooks on another nearby base.

I had the opportunity to go work at the White House. I chose not to because of the demand that is on your life to work there. As a cook, you are always the first to get up before everyone and the last to go to bed. I didn't want to give up my freedom and dedicate the time that was needed. It would have been a great experience, but I passed it up. I did get to visit inside the White House with my Chief and a few other sailor friends of mine, which was nice to see! I was also stationed there during President Barack Obama's first inauguration in 2009, and I along with a few friends was in the crowd amongst the millions of others.

Being in the military, it is always interesting going to a new duty station. You are the new kid on the block, and everyone wants to know who you are, but there's still that one who sneaks past everyone else. So, there was a certain someone who caught my attention, and we became cool until I found out he was married. He was such a liar. I wasn't even the only girl, besides his wife, in his life. Military men are something else. Trust me; everybody is either married or going through a divorce. I'm not here to bash, but I have seen too many things. Am I saying all military men are dogs? Not at all. That's like saying all men are dogs. I am not a male basher. I know some fantastic, faithful, God-fearing men, who are in the military and love their family. I am just saying it is so easy to cheat and commit adultery that it becomes so routine. So, unless he is God-fearing, then yes, I question him.

I fell victim to dealing with a married man who was still in an active marriage with his wife, and when I found out the truth, I said to myself, the next man I meet, I am going to marry him. In my mind, marriage was the answer, and no man could ever hurt me again because he'll be all mine.

That just goes to show how delusional I was about what a marriage is. I knew I had to get married to have sex, but I had no real understanding of what it took to stay married. One of the other reasons I got married was because we were getting more money, but we were in love, or so we thought. I met him at the church I was attending, and for me, it was love at first sight. I saw someone who was tall (just how I like them), handsome, not in the military, and in church. I thought it doesn't get any better than this.

After getting to know him for a couple of months, we made the decision to get married. No proposal or anything, just, "Let's get married!" Even though we did seek out advice, we didn't follow through with the advice we were given. We asked the Bishop of the church, what was too soon to get married? The fact we had to ask that question should have told us both that we weren't ready. The Bishop asked Robert if he asked me to marry him, he said yeah, then asked did I say yeah, and he said yes, she did. So, the Bishop said, "Ok, but you guys need to get some counseling and talk to someone." He called the Associate Pastor over and asked him to set up an appointment with us. The pastor told us what to do, but we left the church and went and did what we wanted to do.

I had just got to that church in November 2006, Robert just got back in church in January 2007, we started talking in February, and we spoke to the Bishop in March. I just turned twenty-one that April, we went to get a license at the courthouse, and April 20, 2007, we got married in someone's living room. WOW!!!

I look back now and can't believe how ignorant we both were. I choose not to live in regret because I learn from my mistakes, but this is embarrassing. The first few months of being married we got into our first of many fights to come. It got so bad that I ended up in jail. We were fighting outside of our apartments in Alexandria, VA, and some neighbors upstairs saw it. I caught myself calling the police on him, and I get locked up. They said I assaulted him first, which is what the witnesses reported, so they had to take me to jail. I couldn't argue, because it was true. We were arguing in my car, and I wanted him to get out and he wouldn't, so I walked around to the passenger side, trying to snatch him out. He wouldn't move, so I punched him in the face. He's six feet, three inches tall, and I did not care, that didn't scare me. My five-foot, four-inch self-was ready. He got out of the car and punched me in the stomach, and then we were going at it in the parking lot.

Although I was saved, I was still very much a fighter. The Lord hadn't delivered me yet, but it would soon come.

In middle and high school, fighting was almost a hobby for me. I fought any and everybody: boys, girls, and anybody else who got in my way. Now, I was not a bully and didn't start drama. I was just always ready to fight and looked for the opportunity. I didn't win them all either; I got beat up too and was jumped my senior year of high school on my birthday. The fighting was so bad that my principal told my mom that if I was to get in one more fight, I would be expelled from school. My mom was not somebody to play with and I was not about to test that crazy, so I calmed down to get through graduation.

I'm not proud about any of this, but this is what I went through. I know a lot of it was because I was angry. I was mad at my dad for not being there and always lying when he came around. I hated him for a long time. I praise God that we have a great relationship now. Even while he's still in jail, we stay in touch. I go visit him whenever I can. I was mad at my mom for getting and staying in a lesbian relationship and it was embarrassing. I was also the middle child, so I was mad because I felt my mom babied my little brother and because she and my sister had something in common since they did hair together.

I was also mad at my dad's family because I felt they were never there for us. I was mad at my sister because I thought she didn't love me, she always chose her friends over me. I was mad at my brother too for having a baby so young, and now he was a dad and not my baby brother anymore. I just got tired of being hurt, so by fighting, I could defend myself and make the hurt go away. Of course, it was short-term relief, but that was the only way I knew how to cope.

Although I was mad at everyone for my reasons, no one did anything to me personally. I didn't have a mentor or anyone to talk to growing up and had to learn to handle things by myself. Learning how to self-cope is why I'm so independent now and cringe at the thought of having to ask anyone for anything. I can if I need to, but it's hard to do.

I argued with everybody growing up. No one was safe with the mouth I had. Not to give my ex-husband a pass for the things he did to me, but I know my mouth drove that man crazy. I knew what to say to piss him off and get under his skin. I wasn't aware then that that's what I was doing, but deep down I knew what I was doing. The day I got locked up, it was only for seven hours, then he came to get me out. Three months after that incident I got pregnant with our oldest daughter.

The rest of our marriage was filled with fighting, arguing, and disrespect. Robert went to jail a few times behind our fights as well. I had no respect for him, and he had no love for me. I now know how much a man needs respect. I had no idea what respect was, so I couldn't give him what I didn't know. Vice versa: he had no idea how to love me. We were kids trying to do adult things in our early twenties. He's two years older than me, but we were very young mentally. Not to say we couldn't have made it that young, but neither one of us had an example of a stable, healthy marriage growing up.

We separated about three times throughout the time of our marriage, and they were at least six- to eight-month separations. When I was seven months pregnant with our second daughter in January of 2011, the incident occurred that was the final straw for me and that dysfunctional marriage. We were living in Oxnard, California, at the time and got into a horrible argument on a Sunday morning heading to church. After church, he wanted to use my car to go to the gym, and I said no. There were so many reasons that led up to that no. One thing led to another, and he ended up cursing me out at the church in front of one of the pastors and everybody else who witnessed it. I was always called all kinds of names other than a child of God when no one was around, but it scared the crap out of me that he showed out like that in front of people, and in church. To me, it said, he didn't care, and if he didn't care, I was not safe. I was already scared of him at this point because when he gets mad, the only way I could control him was to call the police.

That night, I had already made up in my mind that I was over this marriage with him. By now, I was tired of fighting. I had no more in me to argue, no more strength to fight, just no more energy to keep trying when it was over. On top of this, I was seven months pregnant!

He came home that night, and I wouldn't let him in, so he kicked the front door to the apartments. Thank God my friends the Wilsons were at the house with me. When Robert came to the house I went to the door to see what he wanted, and he said he wanted to use the phone. I never opened the door; we were communicating while it was locked. I asked my friend's husband to go outside with him and let him use his phone. He said cool. I asked Robert to move away from the door, so I could open it.

The whole time I was looking out of the peephole. Robert walked around the corner to act as if he went down the steps. I didn't trust him, so I jiggled the doorknob to see what he was going to do. He ran to the door very sneakily, and I said, "See, I knew it." Next thing I knew, he kicked the door with the sole of his foot, not like kicking a soccer ball. At that first kick, I ran into my daughter's closet in her bedroom and called the police very quietly. At the second kick, he broke in, and all I heard was a bunch of rumbling. My friend's husband was wrestling with him in the hall trying to get him to calm down.

We had just moved in that apartment a week prior. I had had to find a residence outside the base to live in because Robert just got us kicked off base. So, when the police came that night, I broke down in front of them and said I'm tired of calling you all to my house. By this point, this had to be about the 8th or 9th time the police got involved. The police just asked me, "So why do you keep letting him come back?" I stood there with a blank stare and said, "I don't know." But at that moment, I knew it was over. I went to stay with my friends that night and ended up moving back to base about five months later.

As soon as I gave birth to my daughter in March, I was at the courthouse filing for divorce. September 25, 2011, my divorce was final. Again, I live in no regrets because I learn from my mistakes, but if I had any advice to give to anyone, it would be to WAIT ON GOD! I wasn't spiritually mature enough to be picking anyone as my spouse and should have waited on the Lord to pick my husband. I was just a desperate young girl looking for love. Growing up without a father figure opened doors in my life for men to hurt me and I had no defense against them. I didn't have any man to call and cry for help. However, I praise the Lord for teaching me to call on the name of Jesus!

Honestly, Robert wasn't a mean person; his anger just controlled him. When he got mad, he broke things, put holes in walls, threw things, and didn't control himself. I had to escape many times. It took me a long time to forgive him. I mean to forgive him truly. I said before that I forgave him, but every time he called the girls I had an attitude. Most times I drove away from dropping them off with him, and I'd be rolling my eyes. I was just nasty with him anytime we would talk. That's a sign of unforgiveness. Anyone you are still mad at, you haven't forgiven.

I mean it didn't matter if he was nice, I could be nice back, but deep down inside just angry. But God! The Lord recently dealt with me concerning him. It wasn't until about four months before I wrote this chapter that I truly forgave him. I just started praying for him and his salvation one day, and I got delivered through praying for him.

Seven years after letting the marriage go. I believe that's why I'm still single. I couldn't take my bitterness into another relationship; it doesn't work.

The way to forgive someone is to pray for them. You cannot hate someone who's in your prayers. I'm talking about true intercession on their behalf. Two weeks after my prayer, he popped up on the girls for my youngest daughter's birthday after not seeing them for a year and a half, due to me moving to Georgia. He had no idea what took place between God and me, but because of the self-deliverance I went through, it was a pleasant visit. We will never be together again, for more reasons than one, but I know that I'm free from the hurt and pain that took place. Now when he calls the girls, nothing in me gets upset or irritated. I'm just happy we're able to get along for the sake of our girls.

Chapter 5

The Transition

~Learning How to Walk with Faith~

I decided in November 2012 that I was ready to get out of the Navy. I was at a point in my life where the military was no longer fulfilling to me. I felt I was there for a paycheck and it just wasn't worth it anymore. I didn't like my job nor the people who surrounded me. I just didn't want to be in that environment or under the control of the military. I was ready to go and let my wings fly. I even remember saying that when people asked me why I was getting out. I said because I want to live by faith and trust God. Which was right—I just had no idea what I was asking.

Before I made the decision to get out, financially life was good. I had a place to stay, I had a car to drive, we had food in the house, and my kids went to a great daycare. I was in a little debt, but I would have kept making rank and eventually taken care of it. I got out as an E-5 Second Class Petty Officer. The same year I got out, I hit a pay increase, I was eligible for ranking up to E-6 and just got approved to continue in my job. The military started doing this approval or denial process for people having to either re-enlist or get discharged. If you were "needs of the Navy" (meaning they need you), then you could stay, but if they had no more use for you and or the job you were doing, then you got kicked out. They did pay you a nice chunk of severance pay for putting you out on an honorable discharge, but you had to go. They did approve me to stay in, but none of that was enough for me to re-enlist. I wish they had denied me, because that way I would have gotten that money, but not too many things can make me change my mind when it's made up. Unless it's God, and I'm convinced that it's Him.

It was also my time to go on a ship for the next tour. I managed to make it eight years in the Navy without getting stationed on a ship. In the Navy, you must do sea/shore rotations every time you switch duty stations. Although being stationed in California was considered a sea duty for me, it was the C-130 cargo planes that deployed from the squadron that made it a sea duty. Somehow, they realized I needed to go to a ship and would have sent me on back-to-back sea duties. I never wanted to go to the ship before because of the horror stories that I would hear about being a Culinary Specialist on a ship. I wish I hadn't let that scare me and just took the chance. Not that I regret not going, but that is one thing I wish I could have experienced for myself.

I chose not to go to the ship this time because of my children. When you're on the ship, you can get deployed anywhere from six to nine months at a time, and I could not leave my girls for that amount of time. Again, it wasn't worth it to me. I just wanted to get out, work a regular job like everybody else, and live an ordinary life. That's far from what happened. First off, I am not normal, and God has made that very clear to me. I will never fit in and do what everybody else does. I think I've finally accepted that and stop trying to fight against my uniqueness.

As I was preparing to get out of the Navy, I still hadn't quite figured out what to do. I didn't know what field or job I wanted to get into, so I decided to go to school. I didn't want to do traditional college, so I thought to go to cosmetology school. I knew a little something about hair, so I figured it couldn't be that hard. You had to complete sixteen hundred school hours in California, so it could take anywhere from eleven to twelve months. In school, I was able to get unemployment, financial aid, and the G.I. Bill housing allowance from serving at least thirty-six months active duty.

From the looks of things, I would still be making enough money to keep me afloat and not miss a beat with my bills and everything. Well, that is sure not how things panned out. As I was getting out, my unemployment didn't kick in right away, financial aid didn't come until March the following year, and although I received the housing allowance, that wasn't until the following month. I started getting behind at that time, but God still provided, and I was ok for a while.

The hardest part about going to school was not having a babysitter for my girls. It was always a challenge. My oldest daughter was starting kindergarten, and I did have daycare for my baby. The problem was on weekends. Beauty school was Tuesday through Saturday, so every Saturday I was trying to find care. I did have a few consistent people, so that helped, but I was paying for care every time someone watched them for me.

About September of 2013 is when all Hell broke loose! That summer I ended up taking two months out of school because it was getting tough. I was stressed out about quite a few things, and I was ready to give up, but I took the break to get it together and collect my thoughts. When I got back to school, everything that could go wrong, started going wrong.

Due to me taking the break, I didn't get the housing allowance for October or November. My unemployment had stopped. We were waiting for President Obama to approve another extension, which at this point, it would have been my third extension. After waiting about two months for him to make up his mind, he finally decided and denied the continuance. I was now getting further behind on my rent and not sure how to pay the rest of my bills. I was three payments late on my car, so they're calling and threatening me. I had to stop payment on pretty much everything. Thank God, I was receiving food stamps, so we were ok with food for a little bit.

Christmas service of 2013 was the start of a dreadful year to come. I worked so hard with the children at church, getting them ready for the Christmas Play. They were little dancing angels, and all their costumes were in my car. I get me and my girls ready for church that Sunday morning, only to walk outside and find my car gone. They had repossessed my car!

I didn't panic, amazingly; I made a few phone calls and prayed for the best. I called my team at church and told them what happened, and they immediately acted. I thank God for such amazing and talented friends. The church I was in at the time taught me some valuable lessons. One of the biggest things I learned was, "Make it happen." We learned that you don't panic or cry when things don't go right, you figure it out and make it happen.

The girls at church found white sheets, tablecloths, pillowcases, strings and whatever else could be turned in to an angel costume. I was able to find a ride from Kelly, who didn't live that far from me. Although she had already made it to church, she came back to get the girls and me. I am forever grateful to everyone who had a hand in that!

Now, my car just got repossessed, but I didn't have time to stress out or worry about it. When Kelly came to pick us up, I was still trying to figure out how to make these costumes. I asked her to take me to Target so I could see what I could find. I found a few white turtlenecks and spent the last few dollars I had. When I got to church, the girls were just about ready and just needed a few more adjustments.

I not only had to go in front of the church to dance with my little dancers but turn around and sing for the second service. I was on the Praise Team as well and had to dance a second time with the girls, all while keeping a joyful smile on my face. There were two services for the Christmas play. I don't even believe at this point my pastors knew what had happened. Nobody was crazy enough to tell them that we didn't have costumes and the girls couldn't dance. Although I believe they would have understood, that is not something they needed to know. He was getting ready to minister to people who need salvation, so angel costumes were not a priority. I am so grateful we knew how to work under pressure and made it happen. Oh, I should also mention

that the girls were so cute in their sheets and pillowcases!

Chapter 6

The Hardship

~It's Too Much~

The reality of my car getting repossessed didn't hit me until I realized I almost couldn't get another one. I didn't think it'd be that hard to get into something else. I did manage to find a dealership that was willing to work with me. I was honest with them about the repossession, and they allowed me to get something. I have never been a materialistic person, but I do like beautiful things. I ended up getting a 2000 Toyota Camry. The car ran well, but it was much older and not as stylish as what I had before, a

Nissan Murano. Best SUV ever! I will get another SUV, but I'm going to get the Pathfinder for the third row. I love Nissans!

Although they allowed me to get the car, I still had to come up with the money for a down payment. I was able to make it happen. I borrowed some from my friend and came up with the rest. I got the car in January 2014.

Living in California was not a game. Where I was living was about twenty minutes away from my church. My rent at the time was one thousand, seven hundred and fifty dollars, for a two-bedroom apartment. If you live there, that is normal, but when you are not from there, that is too much. I honestly don't believe you can live there without faith or family. I was able to get the housing allowance for the next couple of months but couldn't catch all the way up with my bills, so by March I was getting evicted.

Now, beauty school was coming to an end, and I completed my sixteen hundred hours in January and graduated. Around the time I finished, I was trying to figure out what to do next. Getting a job was out of the question only because I couldn't find something that was paying enough for me to afford to live there by myself. I still had about two years left with my G.I. Bill, so going back to school it was. I only went to school to get the housing allowance.

The month of January I was going to two schools at the same time. At this point, I was overwhelmed because I knew I didn't have the money for rent, these new car notes and everything else, but I was still holding on to my faith and trusting God to take care of us. I know God was with me at the time. I have never considered suicide, but for the first time in my life, I was able to understand why people do that. Life is no joke and will cause you to lose your mind. The only reason I didn't give up is that my hope was in Jesus and as hard as it was I kept going forward.

At this time, my brother came down to stay with me for the second time. I don't believe in coincidence or accidents. I am a witness to tell you that when you let go and let God, He will turn situations around. I had a second chance to move my brother with me when I was living in California. Without hesitation, he came and was ready to surrender. The difference this time is that I was on my face before God crying out for my brother and his salvation, way before he stepped foot in Cali. The table and atmosphere were set for him to surrender. My prayers were that God would deliver him from that street life and allow me to serve with him.

I know everything happens in divine order and nothing happens by chance. My brother came down right smack in the middle of my hardest season. I tell him to this day that I went through what I went through, not just for me but for him. I believe God was proving to my brother how faithful He is. Because I didn't lose faith, my brother got a chance to see me in my struggle and never break, but also see God move in some miraculous ways. I was mature enough in the Lord to know that what I did would affect him, so I stayed steady most of the time because of him. When I did cry and got broken down, it wasn't in front of him. All he knew is I kept saying God is with us and he's going to take care of us.

There were plenty of times that I wanted to give up and leave expensive California and head back up North. Even going through everything, I had enough sense to know God was up to something and I couldn't leave, because I would be running. I was a runner. When things got hard, I'd move around quickly, but God was doing a new something. I was just tired of the struggle and always wondering where my next dollar was coming from, but through it all, God remained faithful to us and made a way every single time.

Through the midst of this, I was still serving and being faithful in ministry, always taking care of my kids, even going to school still smiling and carrying on. I can say I had the peace of the Lord with me. I know Jesus was up there fighting and interceding on my behalf. I also know God kept me in perfect harmony because I had a prayer life. I was up praying every morning, and even during my confusion, my hope remained in the Lord.

I completed my hours in January for beauty school and had my state board scheduled on Valentine's Day. February came, I went to the state board and passed my exam. I was now a licensed Cosmetologist. Currently, as well, I was getting letters and notices from my leasing office that I need to pay the balance, or I'm going to have to move. I had already started looking for somewhere else to go and found a condo within walking distance from my church.

At the beginning of March, I got this loud knock on my door. It was the sheriff's office serving me eviction paperwork. I grabbed the papers and shook my head. I went ahead and packed and moved out of the apartment. I thank God it didn't get to the point of them putting my stuff out. I left before they could do that. Due to me moving before the court date I didn't have to go to court, and it never went on my record as an eviction, although it left a collection on my credit for the balance of the rent.

When we got to the new place, I realized I couldn't afford to keep the car. Some things needed to be repaired, gas took money, and I needed new tires. I just left it parked for a while and then called them to come to pick it up.

The school that I was going to was about 25 minutes from where we were now living, but I now had to ride two buses there and back, which took about an hour and a half each way. My brother was watching the girls for me, while he was still looking for a job. Things kept getting worse, and I didn't even have bus fare some of the time. One day my brother and I searched the house up and down looking for loose change. We were searching through the couch, looking on the floor, and digging through drawers trying to come up with a dollar and fifty cents for me to get on the bus. I had to humble myself and knock on my neighbor's door to ask for a dollar and twenty-five cents because I only had a quarter. I think she felt bad for me, so she just gave me two dollars.

I remember washing dishes that day and wanting to throw every dish in that house to the floor. I didn't know it at the time, but I felt myself sinking into depression. If it weren't for me going to school that day, I would have gone crazy. If I were ever going to lose it, it would have been that day! When I finally get to school, I felt better. I was in class with some young guys who were class clowns, so they always had me laughing. I know laughter healed me that day. God is so amazing, and He will use anything to get you through.

I was also in a jazz class that semester. The course required you to go to three concerts within the semester that counted towards your overall grade. I was able to go to one gig before I let the car go and couldn't make it to the others, so I ended up failing that class. Thank God that was the only class I ever failed throughout my college years.

My birthday that year was the best and worst of my life. I don't know what it is about my birthday, but it seems always to be that major life events taking place on that infamous day. Anyways, it fell on a Tuesday that year, and we had Bible study, and I just refused to go. I didn't want to be around anybody. I know now that was the enemy. He wants to keep you secluded when you're going through hard times, so he can whisper things and play mind games. That's what was happening. Again, I thank God for the brothers and sisters in Christ that surrounded me.

My leader at the Bible study sent someone to come pick us up, and she was not trying to hear my nonsense. Not only was I broke, but my lights had just gotten turned off, we were down to almost no food, and I was literally at a standstill with God. "What is going on?" I didn't say it out loud, but that is what kept going through my head.

When you don't have money, you learn to get creative with the food that you do have. We didn't have any syrup for waffles, so I used peanut butter. It was surprisingly delicious, and every now and then I still do that.

My lights got cut off twice. The first time, it was for two days and the next time for five days. My birthday happened during the time my lights were off. To give my kids a warm bath I was stealing electricity from my next-door neighbor's outside patio outlets with an extension cord. It's not right, but I had to do what I had to do. I had an electric water pot that boiled water in a few minutes. I mixed it with the cold water to bathe them. I also used the outlet, so they could watch DVDs on the TV while I was at school, and I needed to charge my phone.

My neighbors didn't know because they were never there. We were walking distance from the beach, so that was their vacation condo. They only came when her husband went surfing or something. It was nothing but God that they were home when I asked for bus fare. I said to myself I would pay them for what electricity we used, but I never was able to. I just asked God to forgive me and bless their home for being available for my use.

When we went to Bible study that night, I was blessed and showered with gifts. I got blessed with a cake, and they sang "Happy Birthday" to me. I also received one hundred dollars in the birthday card I received, which is how I got the lights back on. I don't know who said something, and I don't remember telling anybody we didn't have food, but when we left Bible study, I know God was still working. Lola was kind enough to take us home afterward. On the way home, she stopped at the Christian recovery home that the church had and grabbed me three or four huge boxes of food.

As soon as we got in the van from Bible study, I immediately started getting sick and nauseous. I believe it was all hitting me and I stressed myself out so badly that I got sick. As soon as she pulled into the parking lot to my place I threw up all over her van floor. I again am grateful for the people God surrounded me with that season. She just parked the van, and they helped me get in the house. She and my brother went to clean it up and get all the food in the house.

When they left, my brother and I were in the kitchen just looking at the food, and I told him, "See, God got us." All the while in my head I was questioning what the Lord was doing. I also remember ministering to somebody on Facebook in that season telling them that everything will be ok, and God will take care of them.

I know that my faith was so strong in the Lord that although I was battling within my thoughts, I never doubted in my heart that God would provide and take care of us. It just hurts going through it. I've learned that the higher you go to Christ, the less you'll see. When I first got saved, God was showing up and showing out like crazy. I mean He was giving me everything I asked for, I saw my prayers happen right before my eyes.

As He was elevating me to another realm in my faith at that time, He wasn't showing me the results, because He just wanted me to trust Him. I was learning that God loves me even through my struggles, and all that the enemy meant for evil, he is going to turn around for his honor and glory!

Chapter 7

College Life

~Moving Around~

I t was the end of Spring semester, and I was now facing another eviction. While going through all the chaos I never stopped giving of my tithes and offerings at church. We had taken up pledges that year as well for our new building, and I was almost done paying mine off. I didn't have the full amount to pay the rent for June and only had three hundred dollars to my name, so I decided that I would pay towards my pledge and believe God for the rest. I have always heard that you cannot out-give God. The saying goes, "When you're in need, plant a seed." I know it was not only my prayer life that kept me, but I never stopped sowing into the house of God no matter what was going on. So, God came through every time.

The day after I gave the three hundred dollars, I got a phone call that blew my mind. My friend Monique called me out of the blue to tell me she wanted to send me one thousand dollars. Now, Monique and I have been friends since high school, and I have always looked out for her. She had never been able to help me before, so when God used her to come through, it completely caught me off guard.

You should never limit God on how to bless you and who to use to do it. God will use any and everything to bless his children when your faith is in him. Not only did it help me pay the rent, but it helped to pay off the rest of my pledge.

School was now out, and since I didn't go to summer school I didn't get the housing money for the summer, so I was back trying to figure out how to make a living. I chose not to go to the school that summer because I was over it. I honestly debated very hard that summer about leaving California. I felt I only went to school for the money, and the whole semester I was stressed. It just didn't feel worth it. I went to talk to my pastor's wife about it, and she advised me that if going to school was paying the bills, then that's what I should do. I took her advice and prepared to start school in the Fall.

July was the last month I stayed in the condo, and then I had to move. I was honest with my landlord and asked him not to evict me. When I moved there, the condo didn't have a washer, dryer, or refrigerator. So, I told him if he would just let me leave without the hassle of the paperwork then I would let him keep the appliances that I bought. He agreed because that allowed him to raise the rent for the unit, but I had no money to move, no way to show income, and was not sure which way to go.

With only a few days before I had to be out of the unit, I had no idea where we were going. Our Praise Team was practicing out of the Fishers' house in their garage on Thursday evenings. On this Thursday, Lola and Mrs. Fisher noticed something was wrong with me during practice, so afterward they asked me what was wrong. I tried my best to keep it together, but as soon as they said something I broke down and cried my eyes out. I told them what was going on and how I had nowhere to go. I was crying so hard because I knew I couldn't leave California, but I was so determined to stay in God's Will that I was willing to move to a homeless shelter. I started looking into group homes for women and children, and I was looking into different shelters as well and just trying to figure it out. I did find a lovely home for women and children, but they had a rigorous schedule that would have given me a curfew. I couldn't be limited because of the ministry. It's an outreach ministry, and we're always in the streets witnessing and reaching the lost. Also, after church we fellowship. We were either going out to eat or just there talking. There were plenty of nights that my friends and I talked well into the night after our Friday night services. I thank God for the late nights with my girls. Those nights did wonders for my life; they were so needed.

After talking with the ladies after practice, Mrs. Fisher agreed that my girls and I could stay with them rent-free for a month until I figured something out. That gave me such a relief.

I couldn't take my brother with me, so I had to find somewhere for him to go. I contacted one of the ministers of the church and asked if my brother can come to stay with him. He was an older single man and had rooms available that he would rent out. Renting bedrooms in

California is how most people lived, so it is a common thing to rent a room from someone. I was happy he was available when we needed him—another divine moment.

It was time for my brother to start growing in God without my supervision and now walk his own faith journey. My brother had been looking for a job the entire seven months he'd been there, and nothing became available until he moved. He started with a temp agency and eventually got hired on permanently. He was promoted a few times and still works there today. God does work in mysterious ways!

The condo I was living in was a three bedroom, so my brother took his bedroom furniture with him. I sold a few items but gave away most of my furniture. I still had a lot of stuff, so I had to get a storage unit. Downsizing from a three-bedroom condo to now living in a single bedroom with two children was the hardest, most humbling thing ever. Even renting just a room, I was paying no less than five hundred and fifty dollars. After leaving the Fisher's house for that one month, I was no longer living rent free. I wasn't mad about it; I was just happy we had somewhere to go.

That month of August I enrolled in school. I transferred from Ventura College to Oxnard College because it was much closer to everything. They were in the same school district, so it was a smooth transition.

Also, during this time, I got close to one of my most favorite people in the world. My Friend! We literally call each other "Friend." My friend came through for me. Along with a few other people for whom I'm forever grateful, she helped me move all my stuff to storage and get things to the room. I ended up giving her most of my furniture. She was driving an old, beat-up 1998 green Honda Accord. She would let me drop her off at work and I would go do my running around.

That summer I started working at a beauty salon in Camarillo with Ms. Rivers. That was helping me bring in some extra cash too. When I started school all I was thinking about was getting a car. When I got the first payment from my financial aid grant money, I used it as a down payment. I went to this dealership and was honest with them about my recent repo and asked them not to run my credit.

I know God blessed me with the car because I was faithful in my friend's car. He not only blessed me with a car, but I got the same car as her. It was just in much better shape, and it was a 1999 green Honda Accord. We laugh about that to this day. It seemed like God was blessing us in the same ways with everything. I could be here all day explaining the many blessings we received, and situations that we were in that were identical. It's almost creepy, but fantastic at the same time.

After the month at Mrs. Fisher's house, it was time to move again. I was led to reach out to one of the sisters at church about renting a room. She agreed, so we moved with her. I was there for about six months, and then it was time to go. Living with people is not the most natural thing to do. Especially other women. It's just those women issues that we have.

I didn't know where to go, so I called my friend, Friend. She wasn't allowed to have anyone in her apartments because she was living in low-income housing, but she still let us come for a couple of months. I was there from March to May. I started getting the hang of this faith walk, so when it got time for me to leave her house, I hadn't quite figured it out, although I was looking high and low. I was also trying to find my own apartment, but due to the collection that was on my credit it was an automatic denial left and right.

A week before I had to leave, I didn't have a worried bone in my body. I knew God had me. That Sunday evening, we were at life groups and I got a phone call from Lola. She asked me how my living arrangements were coming, and I said well, I need somewhere to go by next weekend. She then asked me if we wanted to move in with her.

I was like, look at God!

She had two teenage daughters and was living in a one-bedroom apartment, but it had a huge living room. She needed help paying the rent and I needed a place to stay, so I turned that living room into a bedroom for the next seven months. We hung sheets up on the ceiling to give some privacy, and we made it work.

Our church had a discipleship home that was called the D-home. Single people would live there and get trained and equipped to do the work of the Lord. Well, the D-home was moving into a bigger house, and the directors called Lola to ask if she and I would like to rent one of the rooms from the four-bedroom home. That way we could get out of the small apartment and help them with the rent over there. It was a massive house in Ventura, California. My brother was living in the D-home at that time, so we ended up together again. There was a total of sixteen people living in that house at one time. Lola and I were the only two women with children, besides the directors who were husband and wife, with their little dog and the rest were men.

The house had a loft upstairs, and three bunk-beds fit in there. The directors had a room, I had a room, Lola had a room, and my brother shared a room with another guy. We made it happen. Since our kids were there, it was no longer called a D-home and just ended up turning into a family home. Most everyone had a job, so you were either working or going to school, and everyone got up and prayed in the mornings before leaving home. We had weekly chores, and everyone pitched in for food. It had its chaotic and dramatic days, but it was a good group of people, and I loved every one of them as my brothers and sisters in Christ.

Even with all this moving around I was doing, I was still going to school and managing to keep my GPA above a 3.0. I was working in different work-study jobs on campus as well. One of the jobs I worked was at a radio station. I learned so much working at that radio station.

One of the significant things I learned was how to build a website. They had me in charge of their social media accounts and updating the site. I had no idea what I was doing, but I'm never one to turn down a challenge. I not only learned about it, but I mastered how to design a website, just one of those things that God used to incorporate into my life today. That experience created the opportunity for me to develop my website. Everything I've been involved in has some way, somehow made an entrance in my life today. Never despise where you are today, because it will benefit you later. Once you accept that, purpose starts to stir up in you and eventually God will birth something so unusual, you'll shock yourself.

Chapter 8

The Shaking

~It's Time to Go~

January of 2016, God started to do a new thing in me. This was my last semester of school, and I was still not entirely sure what I wanted to do with my life afterward. About this time as well is when things started to get shaky in ministry. The ministry I was a part of was very demanding. I was on the Praise Team, a head usher for a while, a greeter, and a teacher once a month for the children's classroom. I was also the worship leader for my Tuesday night Bible study, one of five leaders for our single mom's ministry, a Sunday night life group leader, and one of the head backstage managers, all while not being full-time in ministry.

For a long time, I was able to keep up with that schedule on top of the struggles I was going through with my housing. Honestly, ministry kept me busy and kept my mind off what I was facing, so it had its benefit. However, this season I entered would be what some would call a "burn out." I was burned out!

This semester of school I had to take an extra class to graduate by May. So instead of the regular four classes with twelve credit hours, I am now taking five courses with fifteen credit hours. I realized then that I would have to pull back from ministry so that I could get through this semester and graduate on time. I was also tired of ministry, tired of doing the same things over and over. Tired of the routine and not feeling that I'm doing what I love. I don't know everything, but I know that unless you are doing it from your heart, then it's not useful, and that's where I was.

It wasn't that I didn't enjoy ministry and serving, because anyone who knows me knows I love to serve. That is what I do. I love helping and being there wherever required. I love being needed and being able to make a difference. I just felt I needed a break to recuperate and figure out what I was going to do with my life.

I went to ask my pastor's wife about pulling back from ministry. I made mention that I would like to stay on the Praise Team but pull away from everything else just for a season. She agreed I could pull back, but not from everything. I walked away a bit disappointed because that's not what I wanted. I just respected what she said and tried to be ok with it.

One of the problems in churches is that the pastors see the damage of people stepping down from ministry and finding themselves backsliding and being where they shouldn't. They also experience so much hurt and pain from the departure of people they've supported when no one else would, so I understand that self-protective side of it. However, I was in that ministry for six years at this point, and I felt my pastors didn't know me. I was saved before entering that ministry, and nothing or no one would have stopped me from serving God. So, no matter what I did, God was and will always be my foundation. I felt if I'm going to do something wrong, like sin, it wouldn't be my pastors or my leaders that I'm worried about, but it's the wrath of God that I fear. Although I have high respect for my leaders and don't want to be a disappointment, ultimately it is God to whom I'm accountable.

A few weeks after the initial conversation with my pastor's wife, I couldn't settle in my spirit that I was ok. I tossed and turned, cried, and struggled about what to do. I finally got enough courage to approach her again and say I can't do this anymore; I need a break.

There was a women's retreat that was getting ready to take place in Solvang, California, and all the women were getting ready for the two-day conference. About a week before that meeting, there was another church meeting for all leaders. At that meeting they did a raffle for all the women who had paid off their pledges, to get a free ticket to the conference. I was one of the winners. The women's meeting for the retreat was a week later. I decided I would talk to her that night about stepping down.

As everyone was arriving, I was sitting there contemplating how to say what I wanted to say without sounding rude. As I was sitting there, I was approached by one of the other leaders telling me that I would be her assistant for the once-a-month women's discipleship that was starting in March. I'm sitting there like, really? I just told her flat out that I can't do it. The meeting was over, and I waited for my turn to talk to the pastor's wife. As I got to her, I was terrified about what she's going to say because I had already approached her, and she gave me her take on it, and now I'm back to tell her I can't.

I have come to realize now, that this whole scenario was wrong. Why was I so frightened to approach my spiritual mom about something that's bothering me? I believe a lot of my nervousness was from the high respect that I had for her and I hated to be a disappointment, but I could no longer go on like that. It was now or never.

When I got to her, I just explained that I was incredibly overwhelmed and needed to step down from leadership and from the many other ministries. I also mentioned that I felt I wasn't there for my children as I needed to be, that I thought I was neglecting them and would like to spend more time with them and not in ministry. She just looked at me and slowly said, okay. She then brought up me being the assistant for the women's discipleship, and I said I can't. By this point, I was grabbing my face about to start crying. She stared at me and said, "So you're telling me NO?" I put both of my hands on each one of my jaws and said, "I can't," while also shaking my head no. She nodded a few times and said, "Ok, well don't worry about it, we had a few other girls in mind anyway."

I was standing there confused as to whether I should walk away or not. As she slowly started to turn away from me, I realized that was my cue to get going. I turned around, said my goodbyes to a few people and went to my car. I cried the whole way home that night. I cried because I felt stupid and a bit embarrassed. I was feeling, she's upset at me and there's nothing I can do about it. I was also crying because I was hurt. I stood there pouring my heart out about how overwhelmed I am, and in so many words almost crying out for a break because I'm about to lose my mind, and it was almost like she didn't hear any of that. It was just like because I didn't do what she said then nothing else mattered.

I wrestled with the idea of even going to the women's retreat now. I talked to a few people about going, and they convinced me to go because I had free entry. I was also toiling with the idea of leaving the church period. It was just too much, and I was tired. I figured I could leave after graduation and go from there. I was going to stick it out until I graduated but that came to halt the Sunday before the retreat at church when I was scheduled to sing.

The Praise Team was backstage getting ready to head on stage to sing for praise and worship and was also going to sing a particular song after the preliminaries. It wasn't the first time we sang it, so I did know the song. They had practiced it that Thursday before, but I missed that practice because of an event I had at school that they were well aware of. The Praise Team leader is a bit of a control freak and had to have everything her way, so she told another lady and me not to come back on stage for the song, for missing practice. I looked at her and, in my head, I said I got one better for you. I walked from behind the stage to the other singers, passed my mic to someone else and told her she could sing in my spot. I grabbed my belongings and went to sit with the rest of the congregation and just so happened to see my friend, Friend, and sat with her. I made it all the way through service with a smile on my face. When service was over, I did my usual fellowship and walked right out the door, never to return. I was DONE!

I still managed to make it to the retreat. The first morning was only for leaders, and the other services were for everyone else. I rode up there with my friend, Friend, who's also a leader. When I got there, I was approached by one of the leaders. She said, "You don't want leadership, anymore right? So, you can't be here." There were a few people around and heard her tell me that, and they were extremely upset because of the way she did it. When she said that to me, I looked at her with a smirk on my face and nodded ok.

We couldn't check into the hotel yet because it was too early, so I asked my friend for her car keys to find something to do. I ended up just parking at another hotel around the corner and sat in the parking lot watching a movie on my phone until she called me to come back.

I honestly wasn't mad because that was my confirmation from the Holy Spirit that it was time to leave this church. When she said, you don't want leadership anymore, in my mind, I thought she's right, I don't, which is why I didn't get upset. However, I feel like I went to that retreat to hear a word from God and to see if I'm tripping about wanting to leave or step down from ministry. I was looking for a reason not to go, but never knew the Lord would move so fast.

When I got back to the hotel, I saw my pastor and his wife in the hallway talking to everyone. I spoke as well and then asked my pastor if I could talk to them both sometime that day, just about what I've been feeling and get his take on it. He said ok and kept it moving.

There were about three more hours left before the evening service began, so after everyone checked into their hotel room, we all went to walk around town and grab something to eat. It was a small, beautiful village with all kinds of restaurants and cool stores where you can shop. My group stopped at this candy shop right before heading back to the hotel. As we were in the store, one of the girls noticed our pastors walking past. So, everyone started walking out of the store to speak. When I got outside, my pastor's wife saw me, and we made eye contact, she immediately turned around and started walking. I honestly don't believe she did it on purpose, it was just a reaction, like oh I'm not talking to her, so let me keep going. At that moment, I knew she was upset with me, either about me wanting to step down or maybe someone mentioned to her that I'm leaving.

I did mention to a few people that I was thinking about leaving town and going to another ministry, which is part of the reason why I wanted to talk to them to get their thoughts. I also put two and two together, that she's the one who told them to tell me I couldn't stay at the leadership meeting.

When they assigned everyone to their hotel rooms earlier, I was assigned with the same lady who told me I couldn't be at the meeting. As I said, I wasn't mad at her, because I just felt the Lord gave me the confirmation I needed. Plus, I loved her, and I still do! So, when we got back to the room, I just asked her (I'll call her Brenda) did our pastor's wife know I'm leaving. Brenda said yes, and I'm like well how did she know. I had wanted to talk to them myself and let them know what I was thinking about doing. Right then, it all started making sense. I was now officially hurt and looking for somewhere to cry, yet again. I got dressed for the evening and headed down to the ballroom. So many things were going through my head, I couldn't even think straight. When I got to the ballroom, I saw my backstage manager leader, whom I adore, sitting in the back. I walked over to her, sat down and laid my head on her shoulder and bawled my eyes out. She didn't say anything, she just held me and rubbed my back. I was able to mumble a few words after I stopped crying, but by this time I was over it. The next two days were torture. I was uncomfortable; I couldn't stop crying, I couldn't enjoy myself.

The second day of the retreat was even worse, because my pastor spoke a message and I felt he was talking about me. It just hit too close to what I was going through, and I couldn't shake it. I accepted what he was saying and could only sit there shaking my head to myself ready to go. Not to mention, they never made the time to meet me. When it was time to leave the retreat, my mind was made up about moving, and there was no looking back

I share that situation, not to blast anyone or make anyone look bad, but to tell my story the way it happened to me. It is also another turning point in my life and the reason I am so bold in my walk now. I hope that it doesn't happen to anyone else, and I want to give another perspective on the way ministry can hurt someone if you're not careful. I'm grateful that God chose me to go through it because nothing about what happened caused me to want to walk away from the Lord. People mess up when they blame God for humans merely being humans. No one is perfect, and we are all flawed. That's why I thank God He doesn't give us what we deserve, because I would be on my way to Hell, and so would you.

Although I left the church, I was still in the house with everyone who attended the ministry, so it was awkward at first, but everyone respected me and my decision, and I appreciate them for that. About two months after leaving the church I was led to write the pastors a letter. I wrote them a letter and apologized for leaving so abruptly. I just mentioned that the Lord is taking me forward and I thanked them for everything. I went through my moments, where I would cry randomly just thinking about everything, but I never gave up on God and just spent the next few months asking the Lord for direction and what to do now.

There was even one time I was on my way to pick up my children from their dad, and I started to think about the pastor's wife and felt myself getting mad and started crying. I pulled my car off to the side of the road and started praying against the spirit of anger and bitterness. I refused to get bitter at her or the church. I immediately began speaking blessings and favor over their ministry and asked God to provide all their needs. I kept a check on my heart and made sure I didn't hold on to anything that would stop me from going forward. I would even text her now and then and tell her, "I love you!" and I meant it too. Although I went through that with them, it doesn't change what they have done for me. I am and will always be grateful for that season.

On the last day of the retreat, a few people saw how distraught I was and reached out to me. After talking to one of the girls, she invited me to a Tuesday night Bible study that she and her husband attended at a pastor's house. They were also in the transition of leaving the ministry. I took her up on her offer and participated in the Bible study. Those Tuesday night Bible studies made all the difference in my life. The pastors loved me back to life. I really feel that God used them to love me healed, if that makes sense. Their open arms to me as a stranger was nothing short of God's glory. I love them so much for everything they did for my girls and me in such a short time. That just goes to show no matter how long you've been in God, we all need to be loved. I'd been serving God going on ten years during this time, yet their love and compassion was the mercy of God's love for me.

Although I didn't physically go to church on Sundays, I would watch online services from a church I was following in Los Angeles called The Potter's House at One LA, where Pastor Touré and Sarah Jakes Roberts are pastors. Their online services, the Tuesday night Bible studies, and me praying and seeking God like never before is what kept me spiritually grounded.

The Lord also began opening doors that blew my mind. Right after the retreat, it was laid on my heart to get another car. I was helping my brother get back and forth to work in my little car, but it was just hard for him always asking for a ride somewhere. So, I figured if I get another car I can give him the Honda. The Honda was paid off a year after I got it, so he wouldn't have to worry about car payments, only insurance and the maintenance of the car. When I went to apply for the car, they were asking for too much for me to put down but gave me the option of a co-signer and explained that it would help with my down payment. Since I had lost everything in 2013-2014, my credit was shot. I shouldn't have been approved for anything. I talked to my brother about co-signing with me, and the trade-off would be I'd give him the Honda. He agreed, so we went back to the dealership. After adding him on the application, it not only lowered the down payment, little to nothing, but they also said I didn't have to provide proof of income. Since I was in school, my financial aid was not enough to show evidence anyways, so the Lord miraculously made a way. I drove away in a 2012 Hyundai Sonata with only twenty-eight thousand miles on it!

It may have taken some hard trials for the Lord to move me forward, but nothing was going to stop me from serving my master, King Jesus! God allowed me to be in California to get trained and equipped for what's to come. From the words of gospel recording artist, Ms. Jekalyn Carr in her song, "Greater Is Coming"

"I feel a shaking in the spirit,

I feel a beating in the spirit,

I feel a pressing in the spirit,

Preparing me for greater…

If it had not been for the shaking,

I never would have been ready for the making,

If it had not been for the beating,

I would have never knew how anointed I would be,

If it had not been for the pressing

I wouldn't be able to walk into my destiny,

He's preparing me, preparing me, preparing me for greater."

Chapter 9

Faith Move

~New Season~

Graduation was approaching soon, and I was still not sure where to go. I knew that my time in Oxnard, California was coming to an end, not only because I had left that ministry but also because my G.I. Bill was coming to an end. At the end of that semester, I would have exhausted my benefits and could no longer receive the other government benefits from going to school. It was just time.

I was now stuck between either going back home or moving to Los Angeles, CA. In the month of April, I started getting the strangest feeling about Georgia. The only explanation for that feeling was just

my sensitivity to the Holy Spirit. I don't have family in Georgia and have only visited Atlanta, GA a couple times to see friends. It was such a random thing that I was just crazy enough to believe it was God.

At the radio station, one of the ladies I worked with was an artist manager. Around that time, she flew in one of her artists from Virginia to do a couple of shows in the area. I got the chance to meet with him and chat for a little bit. In one of our conversations, we were randomly talking about moving to different places. He was saying he wanted to move to Cali and I was saying I'm ready to leave. I commented to him about how I felt like I wanted to move to Georgia. He looked at me and said, "Why not?" I was like, right, why not. Ever since that little tug, the Lord started pouring down the confirmations. Every time I turned around, there was something about Georgia coming up. So, I decided Georgia it is.

In my head, I thought I would move to Atlanta. There was a church out there called The Gathering Oasis, where the pastors are Cornelius and Heather Lindsey. I have followed Mrs. Heather Lindsey on YouTube for some years and knew about their church in Atlanta. I also had an aunt who lived not too far from Atlanta. She's not my blood aunt, but my family met her family when we first moved to South Bend. We grew up with her kids, so we've adopted titles of cousins. I figured I could stay with her until I got a job and was able to afford a place for me and the girls.

Well, God had other plans in store for me. That summer as I was preparing to leave, Mrs. Heather Lindsey was having her annual Pinky Promise conference in Atlanta. I felt that would be a perfect time for me to go and network with some people. So, I planned to come to the conference, visit my aunt and go to Augusta, GA so the girls can visit their dad's family who lives there. Augusta is about a two-hour drive from ATL.

As I was getting ready for this transition, I let my family know what was going on. My sister called me and asked if she could get my girls. She said she'd keep them for me until I got situated and settled.

Through this process, I learned a valuable lesson: God will always provide the right resources when you're following him. When you follow the Lord in obedience, He is sure to meet you every step of the way. Whatever you are needing or lacking in your transition, the Lord will provide! So, I made the arrangements for us to travel to Georgia by plane, then fly to Indiana for me to drop the girls off, then for me to fly back to California

to get my car, then drive to Georgia.

As I was packing my items in California, I was not sure what to do with all the things in storage. I was trying to figure out how to travel across the country with all this stuff by myself. By this time, it had been about two years since I'd used anything in there, besides a few things here and there. I finally figured I hadn't used this stuff in a few years, so I don't need it. The Lord then spoke to me saying, if it doesn't fit in your car, don't take it, and that's what I did. I did a complete overhaul in that storage. I sold a very few things but threw away or gave away most of it. I posted on a few sites and sent out text messages to whoever wanted to come and grab that stuff. I was so happy when I finally cleaned it out, I felt free and ready to move forward! My amazing pastors where I went to Tuesday night Bible study allowed me to leave my car, once packed, in their garage until I got back.

It was such a bittersweet moment leaving California. I was leaving friends who had become the only family I've known for my time there. I was leaving my brother who I had practically raised the last three years. He doesn't know it, but I call him my son; I was leaving my son out there by himself. He honestly was the hardest reason why I struggled to leave the church and leave California altogether. I literally would cry when I thought about it. I was like Lord, I can't leave my brother. I helped him understand he didn't have to leave with me if he felt God was keeping him there. I just wanted him to be in God's will always. I don't care where he worships if he's following God's lead and not man's. Although he had been in the loop about what was going on, I never told him details of what happened to me, just that the Lord is moving me forward. I was always sensitive to his walk with God and knew that the decisions I made could either make or break his journey. So, I tried my hardest to watch what I did and said around him. If he ever felt some way about me leaving, he'd never tell me, because he's too cool for that. I just asked the Lord to give me peace about leaving him. God spoke to me one day and said, I can take care of my son better than you can. That was all the confirmation I needed to walk away with no regrets.

When the girls and I got to Atlanta, I was unable to get in touch with my aunt for whatever reason, so I had to cut the visit with her and head to Augusta. After the conference that Sunday, I called the girls' aunt and let her know we'd be coming sooner than planned, which made our visit in Augusta two weeks long.

God is so strategic in everything He does. Therefore, you must learn to flow with life. When things don't go as planned, how do you handle it? Are you frustrated? Do you take your anger out on people? Do you give up? Or do you roll with it? If you do anything else besides roll with it, you will miss God every time. When things are out of your control, ask God for direction and trust His lead. I didn't know the reason for visiting Augusta for two weeks. I only planned a few days, but it made all the difference in my final decisions.

We went to Augusta and stayed with the Millers, the girls' dad's brother and his wife along with their children. While there, I was able to visit their church for two Tuesdays and a Sunday. The Senior Pastor/Father of the house was on a trip to Africa, preaching and teaching, so I didn't get to meet him. However, what I witnessed in that ministry was nothing short of amazing. The Holy Spirit was evident, and you could feel the love of God in that place. It's an apostolic ministry, so there was nothing traditional about it.

Every Sunday morning the entire church read their mission statement. I am a big advocate for vision. If you don't have a mission and/or image for what you're doing, then you're not serious about life. As the church was reading the mission statement, my heart started getting stirred about staying in Augusta. It's a fivefold ministry, so there are Apostles, Prophets, Evangelists, Pastors, and Teachers. One of the ordained Teachers was preaching that Sunday in the absence of the Senior Pastor, who is a Chief Apostle.

As she was speaking, she had a demonstration with three roses to show the church. She explained that one day someone picked a rose in the middle of a rainstorm and went on to explain how the rose still bloomed and blossomed so beautifully during the storm. The person who brought her the rose gave her that scenario. She was going

95

through a tough time, so it meant the world to her. She in return wanted to give the rose to three women in the congregation and explained how they were still blooming and blossoming despite the storm. When it was time for her to give the roses, my heart was beating so fast because I wasn't sure if I wanted one or not. She gave the two roses out and then walked behind the section I was sitting and walked up on me and gave me a rose. I lost it!!!

I couldn't stop crying! I felt I had just gone through the worst season of my life, in the last couple of years and the earlier part of that year. Yet, through it all, God was still validating me and showing me how I am still a beautiful rose no matter what. As I was sitting there crying, one of the Apostles was ending the service and asked for the women who received a rose to come to the altar. I could not move. Someone had to grab my hand and lead me to the platform. As soon as I hit the altar, I fell to the floor crying like never before. I could hear him in the pulpit saying, "She is a special rose, she is a special rose." I figured he was talking about me, because no one else was on the floor. I think I was still down there even after service was over. God was doing such a healing in my heart. I had to let go of so much pain and hurt that I had held on to. I never realized how bad it was, but every time I would speak about what took place in my life I was crying. I am a big crybaby, if you haven't noticed by now. Well, I wouldn't say I'm a crybaby for no reason. Crying for me is healing. Once I cry, I feel so much better. The Bible says the Lord bottles up our tears, so I know I have an ocean-sized bottle in heaven.

As we were leaving church, the Apostle was talking to me about coming back to the ministry. He was saying, that's where I needed to be. I didn't get why he was saying that, but I had such a sense of peace about it. I told Amanda Miller that night that I think I'm supposed to stay in Augusta. She just smiled at me, as if she knew something I didn't. It was like they all knew something I didn't. Anyways, that was enough confirmation for me and that's when I made the decision to relocate to Augusta. I still hadn't figured out where I was going to stay or anything; I just knew I was coming back to that church.

After leaving Augusta, we headed to Indiana so that I could get the girls situated with my sister. I got them enrolled in school and helped her move into her new apartment, stayed there for a few days and then flew back to California. I spent a night at my pastor's house and headed out to Georgia the following day. It took me three weeks to get to Georgia. I went on the road trip of my life, and I needed every second of it. I'm a driver, so I don't mind getting on that road. I've been told I'd make a great truck driver!

I first stopped in El Paso, TX to see my God-sister and her husband. I stayed with them for a week. I went horseback riding for the first time, and it scared the life out of me. I started crying as soon as I got to the top of the horse. First, it was too high. Second, I must have watched too many shows where the horses take off. I saw that horse take off while I was on it, flash right before my eyes. So many things went through my mind. Our trailer guide had to steer my horse too; I couldn't do it. After about forty-five minutes I decided to take over. It was a nice ride, but I'm not sure if I'll do it again.

After leaving El Paso, I headed to Houston to visit my cousins, who I hadn't seen since we were little. I stayed one night there, then headed down to New Orleans to visit the Wilsons, who I hadn't seen since they left California a few years prior. They were now stationed in New Orleans. Joe Wilson and I worked together, and that's how I met them. Not too long after moving to California, I not only met them on base, but they were also going to the church I attended, and that's where Cheryl Wilson and I got close.

Going back to New Orleans brought back so many memories. I stayed there for two weeks. The Wilsons played a big part in my life in California. They were with me through all the drama I went through with Robert, and so many other significant events that happened to us both while there. Having great friends that you can hold on to is a blessing, and I still cherish their friendship today!

After leaving New Orleans, finishing the last leg of my drive to Georgia, I arrived in Augusta September 9, 2016! At this point, I still wasn't sure where I was staying, although I was heading to the Millers' house. When I got there, I sat down with them to discuss the living arrangements. I went in talking and saying what I can do and all this extra stuff. Mr. Miller looked at me and said chill, the Lord already spoke to me. I could stay there and not have to pay anything, although I did contribute in other ways. He said to get on my feet for the girls and me. The arrangement I made with my sister was for the girls to stay until Christmas break and I'd be back to get them. That was perfect timing because by then I should have had my own place as well.

Chapter 10

Back on My Feet

~Pursuing My Dreams~

While I was visiting in New Orleans, I was applying for jobs in Augusta and left New Orleans with an interview scheduled for the following Tuesday. I had the interview and was hired to work as a cook on the Army base. The job wasn't bad; it was somewhat like what I did in the Navy but working with a full staff of civilians in a military kitchen is another beast. Besides the little petty things that happened at work, the schedule didn't work for when the girls came back home. I also wasn't making enough money to live on my own. When December came, it was time to pick up the girls. I resigned from the job in hopes of finding something better. I couldn't find anything stable until six months later at the cereal company Kellogg's.

Within that six months, I worked a few temp jobs and enrolled in online school to go after my bachelor's degree. I had also been applying to different apartment complexes for the girls and me. Due to the collection that was still on my credit report, I was getting denied every time. It was such a discouraging process, and I should have been out of the Millers' house by now. What I didn't realize was that the Lord was giving me a time of rest in that season, and I couldn't see it. I felt I should be moving forward and not just sitting and waiting for something to happen. Although I wasn't just sitting, I didn't know how to just chill and take it one day at a time. I was used to having such a busy schedule in California that I felt out of place. God used that time to slow me down and reset my brain, as well as prepare me for the next phase that was coming

Not too long after I started working, I was able to find an apartment complex that is a second-chance unit. They allow you to stay there even with bad credit, but you must pay a nonrefundable risk fee up front. June 19, 2017 was one of the best days of my life! When I got the keys in my hand, I went to my empty two-bedroom, one bath apartment, laid down on the living room floor and cried yet again! It had been almost three years since I had my own space and I just couldn't stop thanking God for His faithfulness. Not complaining through the process, humbling myself to live with people, living in this house and that house all for God to get the glory! The girls were still at daycare, so I surprised them after picking them up. Bringing a smile to my babies' faces made it all worth it. When they came in, they ran and screamed through the entire apartment while Amanda and I stood there watching them and tearing up.

I moved into that apartment with not a piece of furniture, but I was just happy to have somewhere I could call home! I got blessed with a few things that I needed right away, like an air mattress, a comforter set, some towels, and a few dishes. In January of that year, I adopted one of the ladies from my church as my mentor. I admired her walk with God and how her love for the Lord was as strong as mine. I used to (and still do) watch and want to be like her. She preaches and teaches like no one's business. We would meet like once a week, and she helped me understand where the Lord had me in this season.

After about three months of sleeping on an air mattress, the Lord came through once again for your girl. I got up one day and start hanging up pictures in my living room. I got tired of seeing them on the floor in the bag, so I started decorating with what I had and tried to make a home for the girls and me. As I was hanging up the last few things, my mentor called me to ask if I was at home. She had put out the message to people she knew and asked who had furniture they're willing to give away to a single mom. That day, my entire apartment got furnished!

I was blessed with a living room set, a dining room set, a bunk bed for the girls, and a queen size bed frame with the mattress for myself. This is some nice furniture too, nothing cheap. A few months later, my friend was moving and had dressers for us and an extra T.V. for the girl's room. The Lord provided! My entire apartment was furnished in six months of me living there and I didn't pay for anything. Everything the enemy stole from me was returned double fold, and God was not done.

I worked at Kellogg's for seven months until I realized it's time to go after my dreams. I was now ready to step out on faith again and this time put my full trust in God. While working there, the job wasn't hard, but we worked long hours and for not enough money. You worked twelve-hour days and could work anywhere from thirty-six to seventy-two hours in one week. I was doing that along with full-time online school and raising my babies. Something had to give. I dropped out of school and figured I'd pick it back up. I felt terrible about stopping school because I'm not a quitter and I finish everything I start.

In November my pastor was prophesying in Tuesday night Bible study service and made the comment to me to go back to school. I never told him I quit the online school or knew if he even knew I was entertaining school. Whatever the reason, I knew it was God. That word satisfied my heart and gave me such peace. I went the very next day and start my research on Augusta schools. When he spoke it to me, the Lord gave me the major right then; Business Management. I made the necessary steps and started the process for enrollment to Augusta University.

I resigned from the job in December, while waiting for my acceptance letter from the University. You heard me right: I quit before I was accepted. Class started January 4th of 2018 for the Spring semester; it was now January 2nd and I still had not heard anything from the school. I called that morning and asked about my application. I got accepted! I was sent an email of my next steps and how to log on to the school portal. The fantastic thing about it, was the portal looked the same as when I went to school to in California, so I knew exactly how to navigate through it.

The site had the classes I needed to graduate. I stayed up until two o'clock in the morning trying to figure out my schedule for the semester. The next day I went to meet with an academic counselor to go over my courses. She was very impressed with how I picked my classes and confirmed that I should graduate Spring of 2020. I also went to meet with financial aid to discuss my aid package. I qualified for the maximum amount you can receive for going to school. That payout paid all my bills for the rest of the school year.

A few months later, I applied for my kids to attend a private school, knowing I couldn't afford it, and faith stepped in again. Them attending a Christian Private school has always been a sincere desire. They not only got accepted but also received a 90% scholarship a piece.

I decided to write this book and share this story of my life for one reason and one reason only: to make the Lord's name great! Jesus is real, and He will cover you until you recover. I am not a grudge holder or regretful person. I am just grateful that I can learn from my mistakes and not have to take the same test over again. God makes no mistakes; I'm just happy He's allowed me to live to tell this story. I won't end this book by saying "The End" because it's not, it is only the beginning!

At the beginning of the Spring semester the Lord started showing me visions and dreams of my life and I took that step of faith to now follow those visions. That is when *Tujuana Motivates* was born. In December of 2016, right before picking up my girls from my sister, I made my first real vision board with pictures and a bunch of "I AM" statements on them. It has been only a year and a half since that time, and I already see these things come to pass. This book is one of them.

"I am an author" is one of my affirmations that I repeated over and over, and I believed it with all my heart.

I haven't arrived by any means, but I am well on my way. I forgive me, I love me, I trust me, I believe in me, and I am proud of me! You should, too, for yourself. When you know who you are, there is nothing impossible for you. No matter what you've done or have been through, God can and will bring you out. Don't give up on Him, because He will never give up on you!

Affirmations

What are affirmations? Verbally or orally confirming something to be true. It is just a YES to what you believe. The more you say it, the more you believe it. Say them every day with belief, or it's pointless. The feeling you have behind what you're saying determines the outcome. Not just repeating words over and over. You will get solutions along the way on how to accomplish or be the very thing you are stating. I'm going to give you a few positive affirmations that I use myself. Let this be a start but add your own and start strengthening yourself today.

- ➢ I am healed
- ➢ I am whole
- ➢ I am happy
- ➢ I am free
- ➢ I am strong
- ➢ I am love
- ➢ I am peace
- ➢ I am able

> _____

> _____

> _____

> _____

> _____

> _____

> _____

> _____

> _____

> _____

> _____

> _____

My Prayer for You

Father God, I come to you on this day in the name of Jesus Christ and ask that you will bless every reader of this book. Father, I pray that they walk away from this book blessed and encouraged to keep trusting you daily. Father, I ask that you refresh where refreshing is needed, that you will heal where healing is needed, that you will love where love is needed, that you will empower where strength is necessary, that you will comfort where there's a broken heart.

Father, I thank you for the testimony you have given me to share with your people. I pray that each person that have received my words will take away something that will help them in their walk with you. I cancel every assignment of the enemy in the name of Jesus from discouragement, lack, poverty, low self-esteem, doubt, defeat, depression, suicide, and every other thing that is not like you. I speak peace, love, joy, comfort, healing, restoration, and reconciliation where needed. I thank you for the sacrifice and obedience of we your people. Father, we thank you for your patience with us and all our shortcomings. We thank you for your mercy, grace and favor that rest on our lives.

Father we don't claim to be or try to act perfect, we are sinners saved by your grace. We need you every day and ask you right now for forgiveness of any sin knowingly and unknowingly that we have committed in your sight.

Daddy, I am absolutely nothing without you, and it is only by your might and power that I can write this book and be as open as you've allowed me to be. I take no credit for my life and what's to come. If you continue to grant me access to live on this planet we call earth; I will forever give your name the honor, glory and the praise. I will never be ashamed of you and what you have done for me. I love you with all my heart and beyond. Continue to have your way in my life, and I will always be ready to serve wherever you need me. Thank you for loving me through it all, you are worthy to be praised, in Jesus mighty name I/we pray, Amen and Amen!

> I am a Fighter

> I am a Faith Walker

> I Walk with Faith

About the Author

Tujuana was born in Chicago, Illinois where she and her family lived until she was nine years old. Her mother; Ms. Evelyn Hilliard, decided that Chicago was not the safest place to raise her children, so she packed them up and moved to South Bend, Indiana. Her dad, Mr. Gregory Hilliard Sr. was living a reckless life on the streets of Chicago, doing drugs and carry on, which was another reason Ms. Hilliard left Chicago. She has an older sister and a younger brother, making her the middle child. Tujuana struggled to fit in all her life (later discovering God has always set her apart, and she was never meant to fit in).

Although she has always been a leader and never the one to back down from anyone, that same fighting spirit almost cost her, her high school diploma. One more fight and she was getting kicked out of school her senior year. Joining the United States Navy at the age of eighteen to follow in her big sister's footsteps, was the turning point in her life. After entering the Navy and serving for a year and a half, she met a man named Jesus! Jesus rescued her and gave her a real reason to live.

Tujuana is a Navy veteran after serving eight years in the military. Since taking a leap of Faith to get out, she has earned a Cosmetology license and two Associate degrees. One in Arts and Humanities and the other in Behavioral and Health Sciences. She now attends Augusta University where she will obtain a bachelor's degree in Business Management by spring of 2020, all while raising her two daughters by herself.

She now attends Greater Faith Ministries of Augusta International in Augusta, Georgia, where she's under the leadership of her Pastors, Chief Apostle Dr. LeMarcus and Senior Prophetess Crystal Hudson. Since moving by Faith to Augusta, Georgia in September 2016, Tujuana has watched God continue to prove himself faithful in her life. She lives a life of absolute Faith and refuses to let fear stop her!

Her favorite and most comforting scripture:

Jeremiah 29:11 New International Version (NIV)

"For I know the plans I have for you, declares the Lord, plans to prosper you and not to harm you, plans to give you hope and a future."

Stay in Touch

Visit my website for social media sites:

www.tujuanamotivates.com

Email: tujuanatalia@gmail.com

To book for speaking engagements please email:

booktujuana@gmail.com or visit website.

If you've enjoyed the book, feel free to leave a review where reviews are accepted, thank you kindly

References

Carr, Jekalyn. "Greater is Coming." *Greater is Coming.* Lunjeal Music Group, 2013. CD.

NIV Bible. (2007). London: Hodder & Stoughton.